ALYOSHA

Daniel Gustafsson

AUGUR PRESS

ALYOSHA

British Library Cataloguing in Publication Data.
A catalogue record for this book is available from
the British Library.

ISBN 978-0-9932182-9-3

First published 2016 by
Augur Press
Delf House
52 Penicuik Road
Roslin
Midlothian EH25 9LH
United Kingdom

Printed by Lightning Source

ALYOSHA

ACKNOWLEDGEMENTS

Many thanks to Emily Harper for the cover image:
Some seeds do flower.

Individual poems have appeared in the following publications:
Anon, Carillon, Decanto, Equinox, First Time, *National Poetry
Anthology* (United Press), Pennine Platform, Rubies in the
Darkness, Scintilla, Sobornost, *The Phoenix Rising from the
Ashes* (Friesen Press), The Tower Journal and *Writing on
Water* (Earlyworks Press).

My sincere thanks to the editors.

Contents

Apology

APOLOGY

It's hard, for poets, to make provision
For the laboured, linear days of prose,
Like it's hard for a priest to envision

A landscape of briars without the rose;
We pass this autumn like a peeling frieze:
Watch for first-flakes to gold-leaf the hedgerows

To fold this moorland in a glowing fleece;
Watch this blackthorn's unthought-of fruition;
To thread a lifetime through moments like these...

CONSTANTINE

If ever strength can aid our mission,
If ever grace resides in sharpened steel,

Place these chisels in our palms, as balm
For broken wills. Our towers crumble,

Our furrows thirst for the poet's quill,
And this kingdom is ripe for revision.

Grant us beauty to cleanse our vision,
That true design may vanquish false powers;

Gild these streets of ours, drain these gutters,
And bring glory to spilt blood, if you can.

To fortify, crown the brow of each man
With this emblem – to lift us, see us through,

Let this be our sign – that golden bird
The linnet's chirp: chi-roo, chi-rho, chi-roo.

ALYOSHA *

I

Of course they break like playthings, these wild boys,
With their thin legs exposed like birch saplings;

You watch them chase each other, raid the sky,
And fall, victims all of scrape or earth-scuff.

With those nimble fingers of yours, you could
Tear a soft strip from the soot-black sky-stuff

To swathe their grazed skin, to soothe them, to calm;
You would, but your brother has bruised your palm

With his piercing questions, stubborn as nails:
Why, why, why? The arbitrary cruelty,

The dark sky's indifference, the child's cry?
He tells you, don't look, don't love, only think!

It's enough to make the world shrink; but he
Is winter's son, and spring is your reply.

* From *The Brothers Karamazov* by Fyodor Dostoyevsky

II

You know our feelings are fractured wings,
Wind-fraught and frail, tarred by thought and earth-bound;

You know it's a battlefield, this playground –
The footpath buried in mud, the old swings

Like a bird's nest in a gale – but you try
To forget, to banish your brother's tease;

Blast him, bless him, he can bore all he likes
With his fiend's temptations, your heart won't fail.

Don't fret or bother much, your touch unveils
Those thawing leaf-buds his pale thought would freeze.

I bet, at each beating of their brittle
Bird's-breasts, your own birch-bark splits a little,

Bleeds like a poppy in bloom; yes, I bet
That's your blood glows on their elbows and knees.

GRAVESIDE FLOWERS

These are fine, curious figures we cut,
Stood at the foot of the grave; in the east

A low fire, a frozen sky above us,
We come unwearied and with glowing face

For the gaze of those who loved and love us;
We come perhaps to pray: to say, at least,

What feeble gestures failed to tell before:
To show ourselves less completely bereft,

Less unfinished, and just a little more
Fulfilled, more fully formed than when they left;

We come undaunted, in snow or shower,
To bow our heads and raise ourselves up tall:

We come to offer what fresh proof we have,
That some seeds do flower beyond the fall.

PEDESTRIAN

The roof-tops, red-brick and asphalt
In a dawn the colour of brass;

Between the last drinks (the hours
Of outpourings and broken glass)

And the first passing of homeless
Or postman, a fierce gale now greets

The breaking day. One lone figure
Braves this fray, plods the floodlit streets:

A pigeon, poor thing, perched on kerb
Like weathercock on a belfry,

A pawn and plaything of the wind;
And how it taunts him, how it treats

The frizzled feathers of his wings
Like paper, like the torn pages

Of a broad-sheet: he reels in it,
He flutters, flops and keels in it,

Wrestles like Jacob with brightness –
Until, in one breath, it lifts him

With such free and sudden lightness
These mortal eyes can't see the strings.

SPRING

The cropped, hunkered copses, back-bent by snows,
The haggard hedgerows and the storm-stung trees;

Ancient all, there are moments when all these
Seem new shapes – of dabbled-paint and child's-play;

Come the weeks of bright gifts – of daffodils,
Of alder-sprig and fragrant elder-spray –

They lighten, though laden with memories
(Near enough) of Arthur's or Alban's day;

They are old – have borne crowns, been shorn of these
And worn down – but glow so in spite of it:

These are rare, but real recurring moments
When the whole gold-greenery, the whole dawn-

Dappled scenery seems dancing, seems drawn
For the sheer and darling delight of it.

A FAREWELL TO PHILOSOPHY

Let me walk down this long path unwitting,
A lover of sounds and sights: let's be done

With doubt, with your school-yard squabbles and hair-
Splitting, your wisdom's distrust of delight.

A few drab weeks ago, this glade lay bare
As thought; now countless blooms embellish it:

The ground is littered with anemones,
And the finches are in flitting and flight;

There is music tonight in these wide boughs,
And I, the hapless fool, shall relish it –

This audacious beauty that knows no bounds
Of reason. For their treason, let the sun

Shame the embittered, and (clime permitting)
Let my love for life be unremitting.

IN ANTICIPATION

I would marry you for your memories:
For the beaches you loved to roam, the foam

Of the bright waves, and the salt-spray on your
Bare legs that blessed you and lent you the seas;

For all the gifts of your girlhood, and more;
I'd marry you for all that came before

And gave the way: for the winds that brought you
Untethered, and the waters that weathered

Your birth; for all the burdens that bore you,
And all the breakers that built you a shore.

I would give you the bounties of boyhood:
All of the birch-woods I loved to explore,

All the gold I've caught with my quill and cork
That I've shored up unknowingly for you.

AN EFFIGY

He knows rest here, but he knows too how peace
Is restless, how love and longing won't cease;

Though his features may be set fast in stone,
His veins and bones remain blessed with fire;

He's known the heart's privation, that lonely
Place where love is self-enclosed, and he knows

There is no such thing as death, but only
The transfiguration of desire;

Don't think this tomb can house, or time can douse
His raptures; in full view of pastures green,

Of river's play with endless skies, his eyes
(Lidless now) see all there is to be seen –

And his spring heart still hungers, like ours,
For meadowsweet and far fields of flowers.

WARTHILL

We live by St John's wort and briar rose,
The barley-fields bring us the four far winds

And the playful pond keeps the heavens close.
It was not we who chose this plot of earth,

It was bequeathed to us, before our birth,
Was tilled for us and sown for our sake –

Across the tapestry of centuries,
This is the pattern our labours take –

And this form, this frayed and threadbare fabric,
Is not ours to unmask or unmake;

Our task is to love, and replenish
The seed: now that we are of the living,

This long-cherished landscape belongs to us
Only in the lasting need of giving.

HEALAUGH

It is good to be here, beneath these wings,
Among these hand-me-downs and holy things;

Here where, flanked by figures of coloured glass,
We pass this door, we tread this ancient floor

On feet familiar with freshest grass;
Where the burnished lamp still burns undeterred

And the light is furnished with fragrant words;
It is good for us to break our fast

On this bread: this spread was laid to outlast
The years, our fears and feuds of reason;

Where rose and lily, poised on altar-stone
With dauntless grace, though frail as flesh and bone

Still hold their place, still field their roving roots,
Still yield their fruits regardless of season.

WORDS

I

There is no truth in self-isolation:
Our lives are unfolded in language

And we languish without conversation;
I am unformed, now as then, won't pretend

My heart knew itself before you spoke it:
There was no heart there before you broke it,

But an effigy that false words defend;
And I will hear no talk about 'essence',

It was only at the kindling presence
Of your soft hands (your fearless finger-tips

That eased the cinders from my ashen lips)
I was even born to thought; only then

As words fought for my palate, fought as friend
With friend, did I begin to comprehend

II

This is the fabric of our passion,
This is how we fashion ourselves, not in

Feats of self-examination, but in
The living furnace of another's voice;

Not in triumphs of autonomous choice,
But in full defeat, each floored flat by each;

I could only turn from my cloven song,
Could only unfasten my faulty grip,

At the burning tip of another's tongue;
What there was of me was only instead

Of me, expectancy, instance of speech,
And what is of me is always ahead

Of me – but within the distance and reach
Of your epistles, of speech and more speech.

AFTERNOON

His cup of tea is tepid now,
Left too long in the brittle pot:

He soaked the leaves, then quite forgot,
As his heart was seized with rapture;

Yes, as fire catches, time passed –
A moment first, a spark of light

Such as only the sparrow's flight
Or the butterfly may capture.

ICON

The storm stills as he shuts the door,
Parts with his staff and his sandals;

And she sits there in the corner,
A tea-stained cloth on the table

As the prayer of his heart foretold;
Above the stump of a candle

Her quiet face is rapt in gold;
He, who has crossed such brutal lands,

Who has passed through the callous hordes,
Treads softly on these creaking boards,

Trembles like her tattered curtains –
For the kiss, the cupped hands, the cure.

THE VEIL

Her face is veiled from chin to brow,
Her lips petals of a red rose

Beneath the finest sheet of snow;
Her features cold like frosted stone

But for a warm breath that flutters.
On pale knees he prostrates himself,

With poor heart he finds promise there
Of a deep, warm breast that utters:

A flame in a mist of incense,
Her sign is faint, his faith immense

There is a wine in every white bone,
A red tongue in every whisper.

TRADITION

One lies down in the roadside shade,
To rest his head on a stone there;

As lark-song scents the summer night,
He sleeping sees the spiral flight

Of their drops and their scaling wings.
Another turns the final blade,

Leaves his book with the fallen figs;
Leaves the shade of this canopy,

This cover of cruciform twigs,
And steps into the dusty glare:

A stark road now, this golden stair,
And no lyre or lark that sings.

STILL LIFE: THE TEA THINGS

I

A tall pot, saucer, and a cup
(Discarded keepsakes, cheaply sold).

A tripod table presents them,
Agleam before a window frame

Which crimson curtains half-enfold.
Nothing disturbs or shifts at all –

Yet the spoon shadows the saucer
Like sundials chart the seasons' fall.

II

The pot is a car-boot purchase –
An ivory queen gone astray –

Yet it's more than precious to us
Who have wounds too deep to display;

We branded ones have seen birches
As pallid as gossamer gowns –

Seen robins, dawn-voiced and ruddy
Like rubies ablaze in their crowns.

III

We will return to this small room,
To this table so neatly laid,

As branches bend through the window
And the red stars glimmer and fade;

We know, by now, how the first cup
Comes thickened and blackened as gall;

And know, this tea on the third day
Flows honeyed and luminous gold.

REVISITED

This vacant, funereal court,
These roses, translucent and sere;

It wasn't chance
But abstinence that brought him here,
And time's un-begged-for attrition;
It was the mind's
Patience, the heart's fast
From it's fickle fare, the slow cession
Of hope, and the dull ache of contrition.

He has been here before;
Comes now, through a rent or fissure
In that thin partition
Of those long, leaden years;
Returns, like an apparition,
From that fast-retreating shore –

He came first
On a fragrant morn, with summer's
Verdant folds full in flower,
Blissful, and blind to all
But the mere moment's lure;
Came later, bent in will
Beneath autumn's moulting bower,
Groping for lost charms,
Combing the dry stalks
By the mottled eye of the moon;
He returns now,
On an early winter's late afternoon –

To these blank panes, wreathed in ivy,
Sun prostrate on the frosted floor,

To resume a broken body
The turning tides may not restore.

        Call him prodigal,
This visitor of the past's effulgence;
Call him a jaded prisoner
Of the seasons' pale dominion;
          But here, in a moment
Time's stony sentries cannot know,
Between last leaves and the first snow,
          He is offered recognition:

Of faults and follies, to be sure;
Of soft hands' fretful play; of slipshod plans
Laid waste; of young hearts' brazen fray;
          But more:
Of a promise
Of a deeper course
And a truer disposition:

In these chipped, irregular flagstones,
These frozen droplets on the fountain-steps –

A firmer hand, a surer foot
And more encompassing vision,
Beyond the self's control;
          Call it providence,
This craftsman's care and precision.

Here, then,
Is an invitation, to enter through
That low door in the wall:
From time's lonely kingdom,
Where nothing lives but all endure,

By leaves low-gleaming on dark trunks,
By lambent flames' long corridors

To that starlit garden,
Where blades of grass are wrought in fire:
To silver spires, bright and brittle as glass.

Here, he is granted a mission:
To accept a neglected gift,
And pay belated tribute
With all he bears and calls his own;
To bequeath
His presence to those absent ones,
And wear on his humbled body
The marks and invocations
Of memories not his alone.

Grasping this rusted handle,
Lending these hinges his weight,

This is more than choice,
The end of decision for decision's sake;
It's the advent of observance,
And his call to repetition.

Ever dawn, never completion
Of the proud heart's passion;
        He must ever cross
This frosted land
With rose in hand, in sweat of face,
From crossroads' untended briars
        To that ordered place:

From all ghosts this fitful mind may fashion;
From these crude, faltering gestures
        To the arduous growth of grace,
As fury fades and grief grows fonder;
From heart's dusty chambers
        To hearts' brighter court,
Where self is less, where love is law,
        And loss is tempered by wonder.

A PORTRAIT

That smile, breaking now in his brittle face
Like a rosebud eased open by a knife,

Is the same he wore as a child, so mild
And defenceless, fearless for the kindness

Of this life; this is him when blessed with sight,
His eyelids freed from the fetters of night

And his cowered heart unfurled. Other times
You'll find him cut off from the world; sometimes

There is a mirror where his eyes should be –
His silent skull at the centre of things,

The spoken world its scant periphery.
This is him, a sleepwalker of a kind,

His feet enthralled by the tide, his frail mind
Always traipsing by the edge of the sea.

SANDCASTLES

I

They came together to this cusp of land:
They roamed carefree, combed the seaweed for shells,

Then shed their footprints further up the sands;
She didn't come here, then, to curse the rains,

The surge or sea-swell, to rinse her salt-stained
Cheek-bones, or to scrub these grains from her hands.

Now some child has raised up a castle here,
A bold attempt at moat and battlements –

Yet another scalp for the tides to claim.
She thinks, as the tears cut grooves in her face,

This crumbling edifice could bear his name:
It was here, this self-same but moving place,

His restless brain must have slipped its moorings,
The reeling picture spilled over its frame.

II

Of course, she has witnessed sea-change before:
She has seen the feat of the full eclipse,

Seen the long lips of the ocean retreat
To erase its love-letters from the shore;

But this is different to a turning wheel,
To think that time itself could turn its heel,

And memories be memories no more;
And she thinks of that other shifting floor,

Of his feet adrift between white-washed walls,
In that other castle; where fears and thoughts

Disperse like flotsam in the foamy squalls,
And photos flounder on the flooded shelf:

Where familiar voices can't force the door,
He is landlocked and secure from himself.

PARABLE

She'd fall, one day, from the order of facts;
They would find her, half-clad, between the acts

Of some home-spun passion-play: she would say,
Where the long night tapers, so paper-thin,

Where the dark plumes shrivel to a moth's wing,
My milk-white skin, my shoulder-blades begin;

And her audience would laugh, would jest her,
Summon their science to taunt and test her,

Then tell her sins to their saner daughters;
She, to prove herself, to loosen the hold

Of the world, be clean of their leering tongues,
Their tales, would take the veil of the waters:

She would strip, fold her slip on the shingles,
Then fall asleep with the lake in her lungs.

HER

This night, as to some travelling salesman
Lost on the moors, she will open her doors

To pain – who will push his counterfeit wares,
But who won't love the rooms, won't touch the food

Her practised hands and famished heart prepare;
And she must endure, now, that long affair

Of hope with the failings of time: must work
To master this hurt, muster the patience

Of her, whose labour spanned some thirty years,
And whose tears gave birth to a world; like her,

She must scrub the floorboards and dust the chairs –
A sleepless grasp on the darkness, her veins

Taut on the bone – until dawn, like a fresh
Pail of milk, will spill itself down the stairs.

HIM

For a tongue that soothes or a kiss that sears,
He will stir the cinders and the red heat

As if sifting the good wheat from the tares
On the heart's threshing floor; he'll sit and stare

At the slow dance through the grate, poised in wait
For a thief's reward or the gift of tears;

Can't be sure, which drops of sweat are the dregs
Of his efforts, and which the angels' share,

But must draw this low tide and drain this cud,
Like him whose hard grains are history's fare,

Whose cupped hands could compass the floods and seas
And whose peace could harrow the earth; like him

He must warm his blood by his father's hearth –
Where the wine is offered, if throats are bared.

DEFENCE OF A DREAMER

I

He collects these splinters, these little bits
Of guessed-at wisdom and whispered clues; but,

He will tell you, even a paper-cut
Can bear witness: that time is a prism

And history is an old cloth that splits
Like a laugh at the seams. He woos these glints

And waits, for this pent-up present to spill
Its brim, the veins of this moment to fill

With a more-than-music, half-remembered
Half-anticipated, attuned to dreams.

You call him a fool and a fantasist,
Say that he broods too much, this alchemist

Of illusion, that torpor soon ensues
And the tail-end of longing will get him.

II

Sure, he may go down dour and deflated,
That melody he moved his marrow to

Dammed-up or dissipated; and he may,
If the cold lips of long nights beset him,

Grow lukewarm, and lose the love that rises;
But, if he courts such crises, just let him:

Let him sculpt his blade, trade his skin for stone;
If he wills, let him wear his waiting thin,

Let him whittle his dream-stuff to the bone –
He may stir some late light from these cinders,

Chip some tinder from his brain's abstractions:
He may coax these feathered hints into flight

Full of true desire: may strike fire
From the flint of these figments and fractions.

FIRE AND WATER

These are moments that burnish and temper:
This cold lake aglow, the blushed skies falling –

And each golden flamelet, borne by these waves
Like a taper, is a symbol and pledge

Of my love, of my labour and calling;
I implore, as this furnace enfolds me,

That this armour of high hopes may hold me,
And I mouth, to these musical embers,

That my malleable mind may remember,
That these moments may mark and may mould me;

I pray this perishing heart won't falter,
That the forces of fashion might spare me,

And I pray that this peace may prepare me
For the passions of anvil and altar.

YURI *

I

The winds that bore your first vowels must have known,
You were born for this; with your bull-finch ways,

With your flame-feathered heart's exaltation,
You were born to baffle this wolfish reign,

To break your wing-beats on the frozen plain
For the sake of some pure formulation.

You fed your boyhood on the moonlit snows
And the starlit steppe gave you leave to stray,

To form your lips on those lyrical hopes
That lungs may stifle and the tongue betray.

Your home was never the imperial tropes,
Nor the tracts of a newspeaking nation,

But the kingdom-come of love's migration
From captive silence to the song of praise.

* From *Doctor Zhivago* by Boris Pasternak

II

To shield your verse from the pack's predations,
Their slogans' enforcement of quietude,

The iron-rattle of their plots and plans,
Their dead-pan utopian platitudes,

You nursed your couplets on the open road –
Its puddles flirting with the peacock-sky,

With its mother-of-pearl conflagrations;
And you'd never enlist with your scalpel,

The quill and chisel of your healing arts,
For their cure-all campaign of negation:

You have witnessed their botched operation,
You have known the ruins and ruts of it,

Seen them slice up this landscape between them
Then roll their red dice for choice cuts of it.

III

Where hoar-frost seizes on the window-panes,
At lawless and howl-haunted latitudes,

You found peace in a candle's oblation;
At the season of fear and privation,

You learnt that language is fire and food,
Is 'Love, my love', is bliss and gratitude –

That life is all muteness and misery
Unless blood is married to metaphor,

Unless the heart-walls and the measured floor
Break open to music and mystery.

That words may breathe now on the open page
Though lips have closed, you bequeathed your poems

To the poor man's wage, to the parable
And the pilgrim's trail, that is history.